AWESOME SUPER SIMPLE
HABITAT PROJECTS

SUPER SIMPLE

WETLAND

PROJECTS

FUN & EASY ANIMAL ENVIRONMENT ACTIVITIES

CAROLYN BERNHARDT

CONSULTING EDITOR, DIANE CRAIG, M.A./READING SPECIALIST

Super Sandcastle

An Imprint of Abdo Publishing
abdopublishing.com

abdopublishing.com

Published by Abdo Publishing, a division of ABDO, PO Box 398166, Minneapolis, Minnesota 55439. Copyright © 2017 by Abdo Consulting Group, Inc. International copyrights reserved in all countries. No part of this book may be reproduced in any form without written permission from the publisher. Super SandCastle™ is a trademark and logo of Abdo Publishing.

Printed in the United States of America, North Mankato, Minnesota
102016
012017

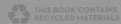
THIS BOOK CONTAINS RECYCLED MATERIALS

Editor: Liz Salzmann
Content Developer: Nancy Tuminelly
Cover and Interior Design and Production: Mighty Media, Inc.
Photo Credits: Mighty Media, Inc.; Shutterstock

The following manufacturers/names appearing in this book are trademarks:
Craft Smart®, Crayola®, Dawn®, Elmer's® Glue-All®, FloraCraft®, Pyrex®, Scribbles®

Publisher's Cataloging-in-Publication Data

Names: Bernhardt, Carolyn, author.
Title: Super simple wetland projects: fun & easy animal environment activities / by Carolyn Bernhardt.
Other titles: Fun & easy animal environment activities | Fun and easy animal environment activities
Description: Minneapolis, MN : Abdo Publishing, 2017. | Series: Awesome super simple habitat projects
Identifiers: LCCN 2016944670 | ISBN 9781680784442 (lib. bdg.) | ISBN 9781680797978 (ebook)
Subjects: LCSH: Habitats--Juvenile literature. | Habitat (Ecology)-- Juvenile literature. | Wetland ecology--Juvenile literature.
Classification: DDC 577.68--dc23
LC record available at http://lccn.loc.gov/2016944670

Super SandCastle™ books are created by a team of professional educators, reading specialists, and content developers around five essential components—phonemic awareness, phonics, vocabulary, text comprehension, and fluency—to assist young readers as they develop reading skills and strategies and increase their general knowledge. All books are written, reviewed, and leveled for guided reading, early reading intervention, and Accelerated Reader™ programs for use in shared, guided, and independent reading and writing activities to support a balanced approach to literacy instruction.

To Adult Helpers

The projects in this book are fun and simple. There are just a few things to remember to keep kids safe. Some projects require the use of sharp objects. Also, kids may be using messy materials such as glue or paint. Make sure they protect their clothes and work surfaces. Review the projects before starting, and be ready to assist when necessary.

CONTENTS

WONDERFULLY
WET!

Have you ever gone swimming in a pond? Did you know you were at a wetland? A wetland is an area that is covered by shallow water part of the time. Ponds, salt marshes, and swamps are all wetlands.

A wetland's water level changes throughout the year. Wetlands can become shallower during dry months. But wetlands can also grow much deeper during wet months.

SHALLOW WETLAND

DEEP WETLAND

WETLAND ANIMALS

Lots of animals live in the world's wetlands. Crocodiles, alligators, muskrats, birds, turtles, frogs, newts, fish, and insects can all be found in wetlands.

ALLIGATOR

INSECT

BIRD

FROG

TURTLE

FISH

WETLAND
BENEFITS

Wetlands are home to many animals. But they are important to all living things, including people! Wetlands are natural water **filters**. They trap pollutants in their soils. This lets cleaner water flow into nearby rivers and lakes.

Wetlands can also protect coastal cities from storms and floods. Wetland areas collect some of the floodwater. And wetland plants slow strong winds. Without wetlands, strong storms would be an even greater danger to these cities.

CITY WETLAND

CLEAN WATER ACTION

Some coastal cities, such as New York City, have saved money by preserving nearby wetlands. These wetlands naturally clean water for the city to use. Using wetlands is less expensive than building wastewater **treatment** plants.

HABITAT
FOOD CHAIN

Every natural **habitat** has a food chain. The food chain shows what each animal eats. When humans harm a habitat, they ruin the food chain's balance. This causes some animals to go hungry.

WETLAND FOOD CHAIN

A food chain has several levels. The animals in one level mostly eat the animals in the level below. But some animals can be on more than one level.

The bottom, or level 1, of a food chain is plants. They make their own food from sunlight, air, and water. Level 2 of a food chain is **herbivores**. Level 3 is **carnivores** that eat herbivores. Level 4 is the top of a food chain. This level is carnivores that eat other carnivores. These animals have few predators.

LEVEL 1

WETLAND PLANTS

bulrushes, cattails, milkweeds, paper birch trees, willow trees

CARING FOR CROCS

Steve Irwin was a conservationist. He worked hard to keep wildlife safe, especially crocodiles. On his television show *The Crocodile Hunter*, Irwin educated viewers about crocodiles and their **habitats**. He saved many crocodiles. And through his efforts, many wetland food chains were returned to a healthy state!

LEVEL 2

WETLAND HERBIVORES

beavers, butterflies, crawfish, ducks, mayflies, muskrats, painted turtles

LEVEL 3

WETLAND CARNIVORES

fish, frogs, herons, loons, ospreys, raccoons, snapping turtles

LEVEL 4

WETLAND CARNIVORES

alligators, crocodiles, river otters

MATERIALS

Here are some of the materials that you will need for the projects in this book.

 AIR-DRY CLAY

 CARDBOARD

 CHENILLE STEMS

 CLEAR PLASTIC BOTTLE

 CLEAR PLASTIC BOX

 CONSTRUCTION PAPER

 COTTON BALLS

 CRAFT FOAM

 DISHWASHING LIQUID

 DUCT TAPE

 FLORAL WIRE

 FOOD COLORING

FUNNEL

GLUE

GOOGLY EYES

HIGHLIGHTERS

MARKERS

MEASURING CUP

MEASURING SPOONS

NEEDLE-NOSE PLIERS

PAINT

PAINTBRUSH

PLASTIC CONTAINER WITH A HINGED LID

POM-POMS

PUFFY PAINT

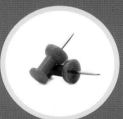

PUSHPINS

SPRING CLOTHESPINS

STYROFOAM BALLS

TOOTHPICKS

TWIGS

BRACKISH
WATER BLEND

MATERIALS: funnel, 2 clear plastic bottles, measuring cup, warm water, measuring spoons, 4 tablespoons salt, yellow & blue food coloring, large clear glass jar, Styrofoam ball, marker, tape

There are freshwater wetlands and saltwater wetlands. But some wetlands have brackish water. This is salt water and fresh water mixed together. Rivers carry fresh water to the ocean. Rising ocean tides push salt water **inland**. When the two types of water meet, the fresh water flows over the salt water. Salt makes water **denser** so the salt water stays on the bottom. The water in the middle becomes brackish.

MAKE WETLAND WATER IN A JAR!

1 Put the funnel in a plastic bottle. Pour 2 cups of warm water into the funnel. Add the salt. Add a few drops of yellow food coloring.

2 Close the bottle. Shake it until the salt **dissolves**. Pour the water into the glass jar. This is the salt water.

③ Put the funnel in the other plastic bottle. Pour 2 cups of warm water into the funnel. Add a few drops of blue food coloring. This is the fresh water.

4 Put the Styrofoam ball in the glass jar on top of the salt water.

⑤ Slowly pour the blue fresh water over the Styrofoam ball.

⑥ The salt water stays on the bottom. The fresh water stays at the top. The green section in the middle is brackish water. Make labels for each section.

COTTON CATTAIL NEST

MATERIALS: twigs, dried grasses & leaves, air-dry clay, newspaper, paint, paintbrush, cotton balls

Cattails are plants that grow in freshwater wetlands. Cattails are mostly found in North America, Europe, and Asia. Some birds line their nests with **fluff** from cattail flowers. And people have used this fluff to fill coats and pillows. Cattails are a source of warmth for many **species** on Earth!

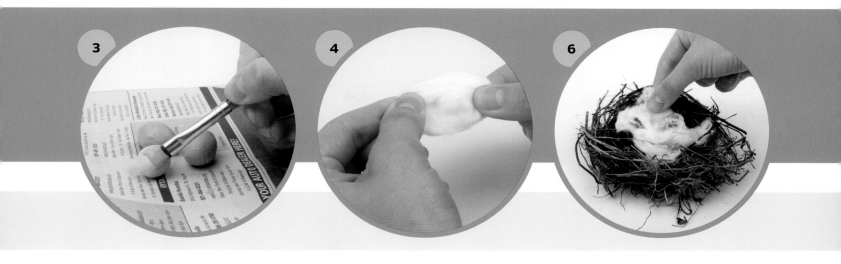

MAKE YOUR OWN BIRD'S NEST!

① Collect twigs, dried grasses, and leaves. Do not pull anything living out of the ground or off of a tree!

② Make a few eggs out of air-dry clay. Let them dry.

③ Cover your work surface with newspaper. Paint the eggs. Let them dry.

④ Pull apart a few cotton balls. This is your cattail flower **fluff**.

⑤ Weave the grasses, twigs, and leaves into a nest shape.

⑥ Line the nest with the cotton.

⑦ Add the eggs and put your nest on display!

SLIMY SWAMP

MATERIALS: clear plastic box, soil, rocks, measuring cup, water, blue food coloring, measuring spoons, dishwashing liquid, spoon, plastic swamp creatures

Swamps are wetland areas between land and large bodies of water. Freshwater swamps are usually **inland**, close to lakes and rivers. Saltwater swamps occur along coasts. Many animals live in swamps. These include crocodiles, snakes, salamanders, and turtles.

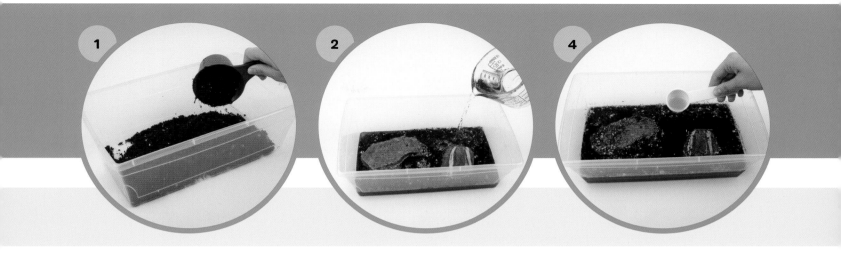

PUT A WETLAND IN A BOX!

1 Cover the bottom of the plastic box with soil. Add the rocks.

2 Pour 4 cups of water into the box.

3 Add a few drops of blue food coloring.

4 Add 3 tablespoons of dishwashing liquid. This will make the water feel slimy. Stir the mixture.

5 Place the swamp creatures in the box. Imagine the animals enjoying their slimy **habitat**!

DIGGING DEEPER

Some swamps and other wetlands can be slimy. This is often caused by algae and other plants growing and **decomposing** in the water.

CROCODILE
FOOD CHAIN

MATERIALS: notebook, pencil, plastic container with a hinged lid, green duct tape, craft foam, scissors, glue, googly eyes, 2 large pom-poms, markers, cardboard, decorations (gems, puffy paint, stickers), string, clear tape

Crocodiles live in both fresh water and brackish water. They are most commonly found in the wetlands of warmer climates. Crocodiles usually eat small animals, such as frogs, snails, insects, crabs, fish, and birds.

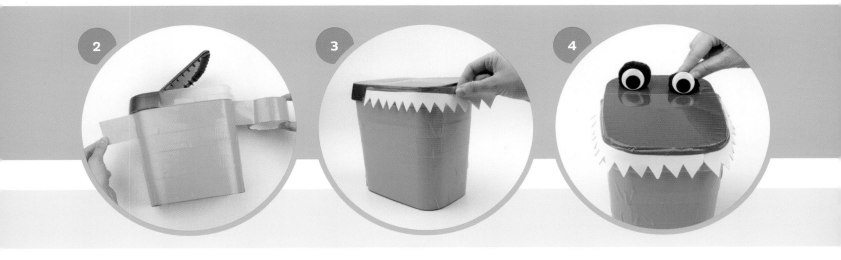

FEED A HUNGRY CROCODILE!

① With adult help, **research** what crocodiles eat. Include what crocodiles' prey eat too. Write it down in a notebook.

② Cover the plastic container with green duct tape. Be sure not to tape the lid shut.

③ Cut a long strip of teeth out of white craft foam. Tape it to the outside edge of the container's lid.

④ Glue a googly eye to each pom-pom. Glue the pom-poms to the container's lid.

⑤ Draw the shapes of the animals from your notes on cardboard. For example, draw a butterfly, a frog, a fish, and a bird. Cut them out.

Continued on the next page.

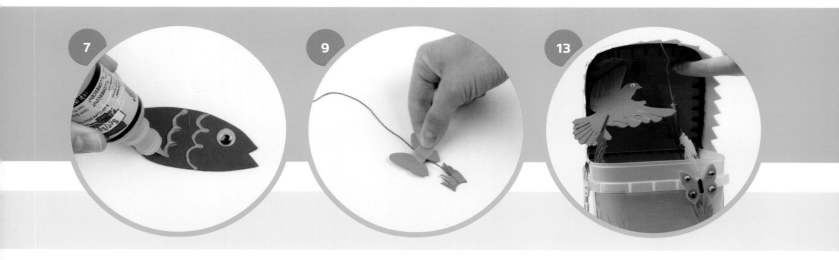

CROCODILE FOOD CHAIN (CONTINUED)

⑥ Trace the animal shapes on craft foam. Cut them out.

⑦ Decorate the craft foam animals.

⑧ Cut a piece of string as long as the container is tall. Cut a grass shape out of green craft foam.

⑨ Tape the grass to one end of the string. Tape the butterfly above the grass.

⑩ Frogs eat butterflies, so tape the frog above the butterfly.

⑪ Continue adding animals in the order of the food chain.

⑫ Repeat steps 5 through 11 to make chains for other animals crocodiles eat.

⑬ Tape the tops of the food chain strings inside the lid.

DIGGING DEEPER

Crocodiles live in warm wetlands in North America, South America, Africa, Asia, and Australia. Crocodiles often lie on land in the sun during the day. They move into the water in the evening. They do most of their hunting at night. There are 14 crocodile **species**. The largest species is the saltwater crocodile. It is the largest living reptile!

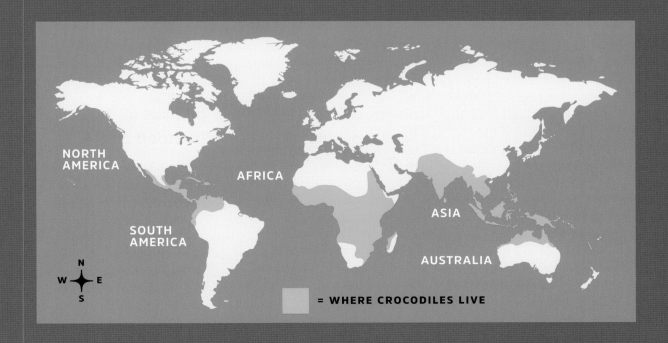

NORTH
AMERICA

AFRICA

ASIA

SOUTH
AMERICA

AUSTRALIA

N
W E
S

= WHERE CROCODILES LIVE

FLOATING
FIREFLY

MATERIALS: clear plastic bottle, newspaper, paint, paintbrush, glue, googly eyes, marker, yellow highlighter, needle-nose pliers, jar, water, funnel, chenille stem, construction paper, scissors, tape, black light (optional)

Fireflies are insects that are often found in wetlands. They are named for their ability to make their bodies glow. A firefly's body gives off flashes of light. The patterns of the flashes can help the firefly find a mate. The light can also warn predators that the firefly doesn't taste good. This helps it avoid being eaten!

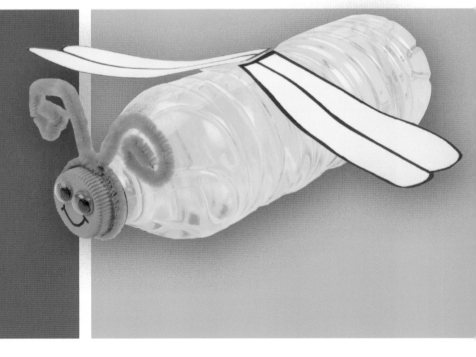

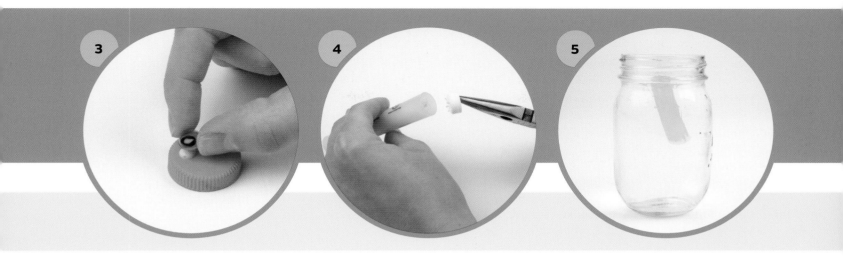

MAKE A FIREFLY THAT GLOWS!

(1) Wash the plastic bottle and remove the label.

(2) Cover your work surface with newspaper. Paint the bottle cap. Let it dry.

(3) Glue googly eyes to the cap. Draw a mouth with marker. This is the firefly's head!

(4) Have an adult help you pull off the bottom of the highlighter with the pliers. Pull out the tube of ink.

(5) Put the ink tube in a jar of water. Leave it there for at least 10 minutes.

(6) Put the funnel in the bottle.

Continued on the next page.

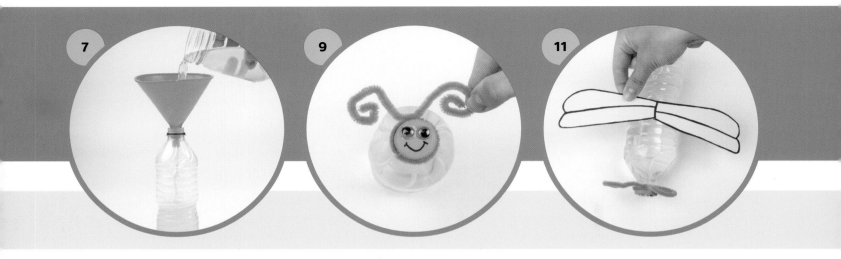

FLOATING FIREFLY (CONTINUED)

7 Use the pliers to remove the ink tube from the jar. Carefully pour the yellow water into the bottle.

8 If the bottle isn't full, add more water. Put the cap on the bottle.

9 Wrap the middle of a chenille stem around the bottle cap. Twist the ends together. Curl each end to look like an antenna.

10 Draw wings on a sheet of construction paper. Cut them out.

11 Tape the wings to the side of the bottle.

12 Turn off the lights and enjoy your glowing firefly! For an even brighter glow, view it under a black light.

A firefly has a special organ at the bottom of its stomach. The cells in this organ have three chemicals. They are ATP, luciferin, and luciferase. These chemicals make the firefly's glow possible. The firefly glows when oxygen enters the **abdomen** through tiny tubes called tracheoles. The oxygen **reacts** with the other chemicals to create light!

FIREFLY

OXYGEN

POND HABITAT

MATERIALS: large clear glass jar, marker, cardboard, scissors, blue paint, paintbrush, brown chenille stems, blue & green toothpicks, craft foam, glue, spring clothespins, floral wire, ruler, pushpin, puffy paint, googly eyes, string, tape, sand or pebbles, plastic wetland animals

Small, shallow lakes are often called ponds. The water in ponds is usually calm because there are few waves. Ponds might be small and quiet but they are full of wildlife!

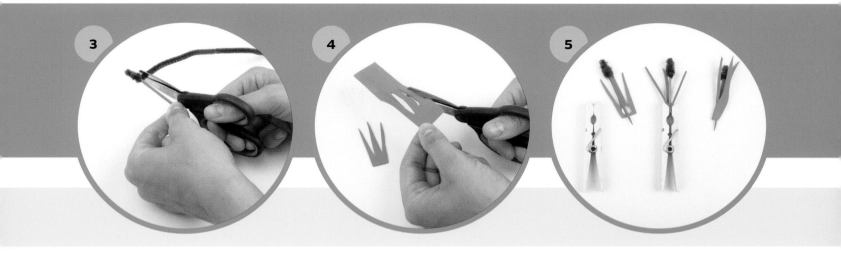

CREATE A MINI POND!

① Trace the bottom of the jar on cardboard. Cut out the circle.

② Paint both sides of the circle blue. This is the pond's surface.

③ Wrap a chenille stem several times around the end of a green toothpick. Cut the extra off.

④ Cut three connected blades of grass out of craft foam. Make them about as tall as the toothpicks.

⑤ Glue the grass around the toothpick. The unwrapped end should stick out below the grass. Hold the grass in place with a clothespin while the glue dries.

⑥ Repeat steps 3 through 5 to make more cattails.

⑦ Cut a lily pad and flower out of craft foam.

Continued on the next page.

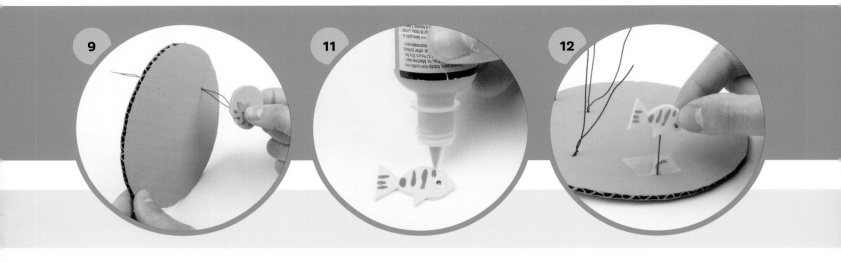

P O N D   H A B I T A T (CONTINUED)

8 Cut a piece of floral wire 8 inches (20 cm) long. Bend it in half. Hold the ends slightly apart and push them through the flower and lily pad. Twist the ends of the wire together.

9 Use a pushpin to make a hole in the cardboard. Push the wires through the hole. Pull until the lily pad is against the pond.

10 Repeat steps 7 through 9 to add more lily pads.

11 Cut some fish out of craft foam. Decorate the fish with puffy paint. Add googly eyes.

12 Cut pieces of string as long as the toothpicks. Tape one end of a string to each fish. Tape the other ends to the bottom of the pond.

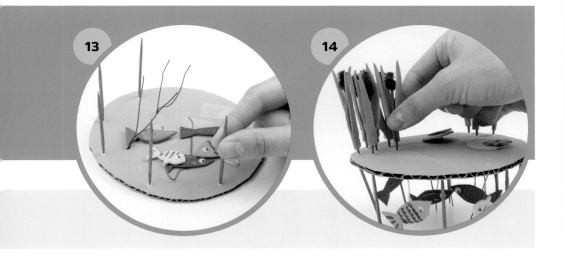

13　Leave the pond upside down. Stick six to eight blue toothpicks around the edge of the pond. Use glue to hold them in place. Let the glue dry.

14　Turn the pond over. Use the pushpin to make holes for the cattails. Put a drop of glue in each hole. Stick a cattail into each hole. Let the glue dry.

15　Put sand or pebbles in the bottom of the jar. Set the pond in the jar. Put a tiny plastic frog on a lily pad! Add other tiny wetland animals.

DIGGING DEEPER

Earth's wetlands are disappearing. People **drain** wetlands for their water supply. Or they build farms or houses on wetlands. The effect of this on animals is often overlooked. Humans are using up the land and water without realizing how important wetlands are to the **environment**.

CONCLUSION

Many interesting plants and creatures live in the world's wetlands. Wetlands also make the world cleaner. Unfortunately, wetlands are being destroyed by human activities. This book is the first step in learning more about wetlands and how to protect them. There is so much more to find out!

Do you live near a wetland? Have you ever visited one? Go to the library to **research** the world's wetlands. Or have an adult help you research wetlands **online**. Learn about what you can do to help preserve wetlands!

QUIZ

1. Steve Irwin's show was called *The Crocodile Eater*.
   TRUE OR FALSE?

2. What is the largest **species** of crocodile?

3. What can a firefly's body do?

GLOSSARY

abdomen – the last section of an insect's body.

carnivore – an animal that eats mainly meat.

decompose – to break down or rot.

dense – having parts packed tightly together.

dissolve – to become part of a liquid.

drain – to remove liquid from something.

environment – nature and everything in it, such as the land, sea, and air.

filter – a device that separates floating matter from the liquid or gas that passes through it.

fluff – pieces of soft, light material, such as wool or cotton.

habitat – the area or environment where a person or animal usually lives.

herbivore – an animal that eats mainly plants.

inland – toward or on land that is not near the coast.

online – connected to the Internet.

react – to change when mixed with another chemical or substance.

research – to find out more about something.

species – a group of related living beings.

treatment – a substance or method used to improve something.